Flip the Flaps

Baby Animals

Hannah Wilson and Nicki Palin

KINGFISHER

NEW YORK

KINGFISHER
LONDON & NEW YORK

Copyright © Kingfisher 2008
Published in the United States by Kingfisher,
175 Fifth Ave., New York, NY 10010
Kingfisher is an imprint of Macmillan Children's Books, London.
All rights reserved.

Distributed in the U.S. and Canada by Macmillan,
175 Fifth Ave., New York, NY 10010

First published in hardback by Kingfisher in 2008
This edition published by Kingfisher in 2012

Library of Congress Cataloging-in-Publication data has been applied for.

ISBN: 978-0-7534-6849-4

Kingfisher books are available for special promotions and premiums.
For details contact: Special Markets Department, Macmillan, 175 Fifth Ave., New York, NY 10010.

For more information, please visit www.kingfisherbooks.com

Printed in China
10 9 8 7 6 5 4 3 2 1
1TR/0412/UTD/LFA/128GEMA

Consultant: David Burnie

Contents

Baby animals

Thousands of baby animals are born every day. Feathery chicks and scaly lizards hatch from eggs. On hot, grassy plains, furry lion cubs and big baby elephants are born.

baby deer

mother elephant

1. Why is a baby deer spotted?

2. Where do baby animals live?

3. What does a baby elephant look like?

Where some baby animals live

Ducklings live in water.

Some baby seals live on ice.

Baby monkeys live in hot jungles.

5

Furry babies

A furry baby animal grows inside its mother's body. When it is born, the baby drinks its mother's milk. The milk helps the young animal grow strong and healthy.

mother koala in a tree

tiger licking her baby

1. A koala
   baby o
   The b
   to take

2. Baby o
   sleep. Y
   also lik

3. A tiger
   to clea
   tiger is

1. How does a koala
   carry her baby?

2. What do baby
   animals do all day?

3. Why does a tiger
   lick her baby?

impanzees

ating

eping

playing

Feathery babies

Baby birds are fluffy, but when they get older, their feathers get stronger. This helps some birds fly, such as owls, and it helps other birds swim underwater such as penguins.

Penguin chicks huddle together to stay warm.

penguin with egg on its feet

8

1. What grows
   inside an egg?

2. What do baby
   birds eat?

3. Who takes care
   of a baby emperor
   penguin?

Owl chicks feeding

hungry owl chicks

adult owl brings a mouse

chicks eat the mouse

Scaly babies

Most baby reptiles, such as crocodiles and turtles, hatch from eggs. Scaly babies are often fully formed and look like tiny adults. They can take care of themselves right away.

baby chameleon

crocodile

1. How does a baby chameleon catch its food?

2. Where are baby turtles born?

3. What does a mother crocodile carry in her mouth?

Baby turtles being born

hatching from eggs

crawling

swimming

11

Water babies

All types of babies live in seas, ponds, and rivers. Some water babies, such as fish, can breathe underwater. Whales, dolphins, and hippopotamuses must swim up to the surface in order to breathe.

baby hippopotamus swimming

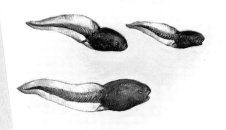

...poles hatch from eggs.

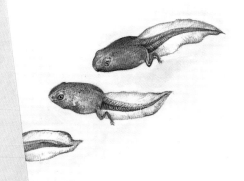

...they grow legs.

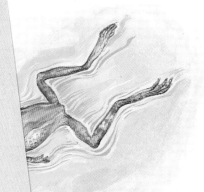

...adpole turns
...a frog.

1. A ...
is b...
in a...

2. A ba...
to lea...
away.
up to ...

3. A tadpo...
legs and ...
Finally, i...
and beco...

1. Where is a baby hippopotamus born?

2. When does a baby hippopotamus learn how to swim?

3. How does a tadpole turn into a frog?

13

Baby homes

Some animals build nests or dig burrows for their babies. Others set up their homes in caves or tree hollows. There are also some animals that keep their babies on their bodies.

baby panda

kangaroo

14

1. Where does a baby panda live?

2. Why do baby rabbits live underground?

3. Who pops out of a pouch?

y panda lives
ive. When it
bigger, it can
utside of the
eat bamboo.

bbits live
und in a
The burrow
n safe
l.

garoo is
. It lives
's pouch
und six

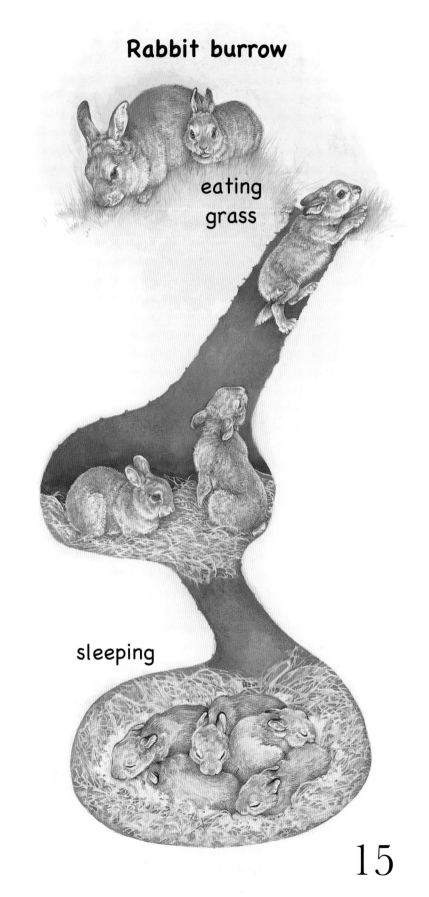

Rabbit burrow

eating grass

sleeping

Growing up

Many baby animals stay
with their mother or group
until they are big enough
to find food for themselves.
They leave when they can
walk, run, or fly well.

**young bears
play-fighting**

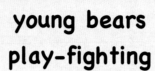

da

16

1. Chicks grow long feathers and flap their wings to make them stronger. Then they try to fly from the nest.

2. A brown bear lives with its mother for three years. It becomes fully grown when it is ten years old.

3. Young bears play-fight because it makes them stronger—and it is fun!

Parrot chicks growing up

Chicks have soft feathers.

They then grow long feathers . . .

and learn to fly!

Index